Perfekti

Diana Ozola

BookLeaf Publishing

India | USA | UK

Presentation by *BookLeaf Publishing*

Web: www.bookleafpub.com

E-mail: info@bookleafpub.com

ISBN: 9789358313093

First edition 2024

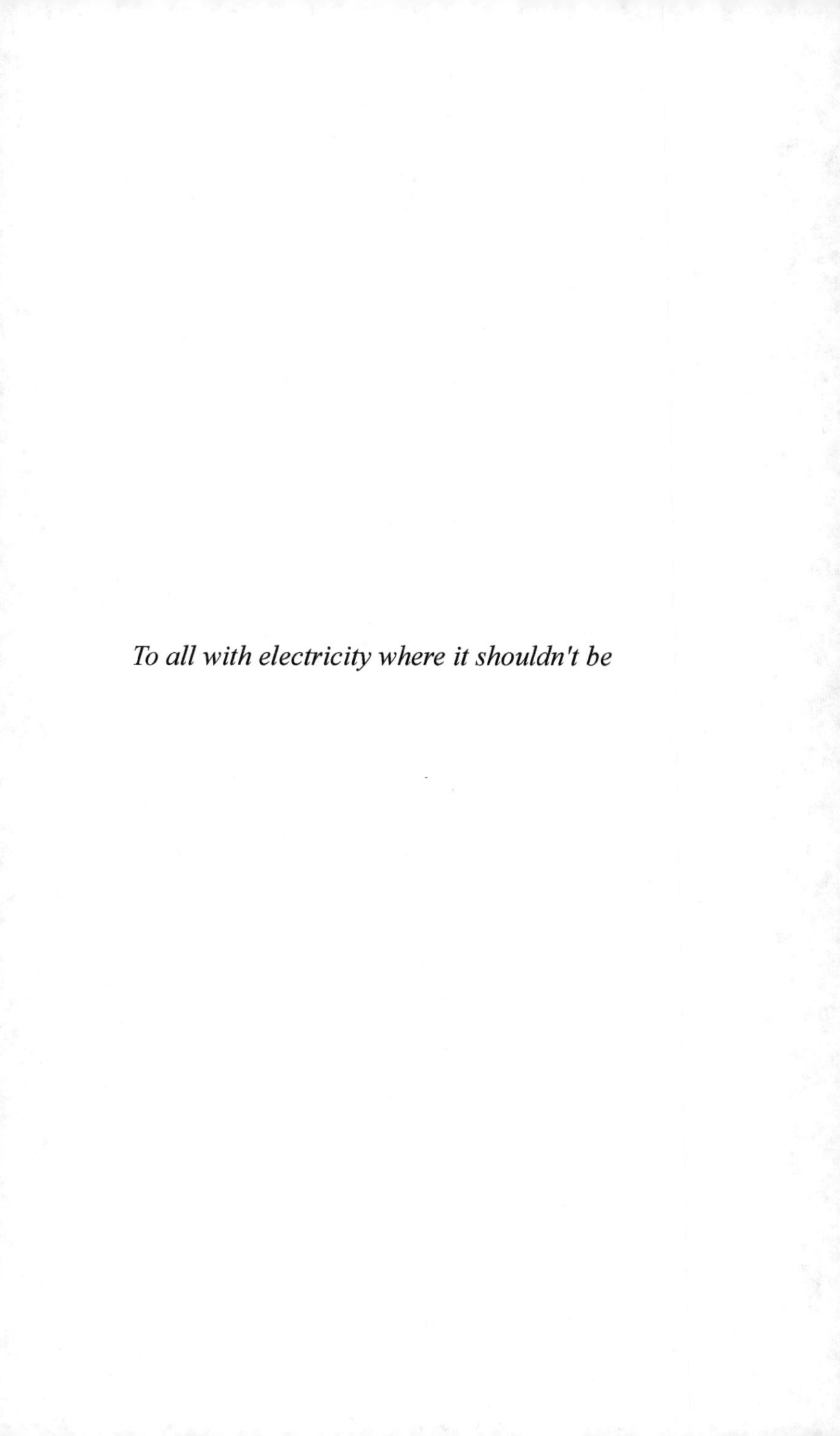

To all with electricity where it shouldn't be

PREFACE

'Perfekti' reflects on my, quite frankly, stupid thought patterns and beliefs in my teen years until an 'arrow' suddenly struck and set me straight.

This arrow was a tonic-clonic seizure in the summer of 2022, which led to my diagnosis of temporal lobe epilepsy, caused by a growth in my temporal lobe. I had just turned seventeen, and my life was flipped upside down. In one aspect, it made sense, seeing as though since the age of thirteen, I had been experiencing sudden 'waves' of emotions and physical sensations that doctors wrote off as panic attacks. It was later found that these were partial focal seizures, or as I refer to them, 'beasts'. At that time, there was not a day that went by that I was not stressed about something, and I now know that I played a big part in this sudden attack.

The partial focal seizures worsened after that summer. Before, they were simply unpleasant sensations that caused unpleasant emotions, or sometimes a feeling of déjà vu. Now, they distort my understanding of what others say to me, and I lose my ability to talk or even form my thoughts. As a writer, I'm sure you can imagine how this is not very handy.

A year on from the diagnosis, I still experience them on an almost daily basis, but as I have grown to understand that stress was my biggest enemy, I have noticed that I only aggravate the beasts when I'm stressed. They are sometimes really strong, to the point I cannot understand anything and feel like I might have another serious seizure. At other times, they are nothing but a little discomfort.

Our thoughts seem to only matter in our minds, but this collection proves otherwise. How you think affects your body, too. There are now many books and articles discussing this, and how I wish I would have read at least one at the height of my anxiety, perfectionism, and desperate need to plan my whole life out ahead of me.

My mother always told me to calm down and let it go, and though I knew I should, I somehow wouldn't, and perhaps I couldn't. It all went in through one ear and out the other. I have only my mother to thank for getting me through this last year. She helped me calm down, kept me in check, and pushed me when I needed to be pushed. I do not know how to even begin to thank her.

The poems transition in the same way my own thinking changed following such a shock: helplessness, anger, fear, and hope. It is difficult to shake such a rigid, toxic mindset, and sometimes it is so deeply ingrained that only something as serious as a seizure can snap you out of it. Therefore, it is through my experience that I now wish to pass on this message to other young people whose default mode is stress. Do what you can, but make time for yourself, your family and your friends. Nothing is more important than that. If it is meant to be, then let it be.

After the first arrow struck, I lost my creative mojo, my will to write for a long time. Perhaps this was in part related, but it is with this collection that I broke free, and found my voice again. My epilepsy is something I had been ashamed to talk about with people outside my family and doctors, but I broke out of this mindset in the process of writing this collection. I realised it is something that is not talked about enough.

Many have a skewed understanding of epilepsy,
as did I before the arrow, thinking it is only
when a person suddenly begins jerking on the
ground with foam around their mouth. Though
this is a common form of seizure, it is not the
case for every person with epilepsy. It is a
spectrum: all seizures are unpredictable, as is
any form of electricity.

I have been reading other people's experiences
of epilepsy, and I have found that a large number
have gone through something very similar to
me. Their first seizure strikes between the ages
of fifteen to eighteen, and it changes almost
everything for them. Of course, causes and
treatments are different, but I have no doubt that
the first weeks are just as terrifying for every
one of us. We are a question to others, and
questions are all we can ask.

It is therefore that I dedicate this collection to all
those who have epilepsy or seizure activity of
any kind. It's not easy, and it's even harder when
you feel like you are the only one.

Perfection

I remember getting in trouble,
for painting on the walls,
for not sharing my chocolates,
for ruling the playground.

But it was the moments
when my praises were sung
from the trees with lanyards,
and there were only green marks on my work,
that screamed into my face,
that I need to be a good girl.

I was free, and I placed the handcuffs on myself.

Second Best

Why do I always need to be the best?
I'm constantly beset with this feeling of
racing and chasing, an unrelievable itch
to be that bitch, sat on the first podium:
gloating silently, shyly hanging my head
to the side, acting as if it came naturally,
as if I didn't spend hours by the books,
as if I didn't have standards of myself,
set so high beyond the farthest of stars,
as if I wasn't afraid to have my heart
burst out of my chest if I achieved
something slightly lower than the best.

The sound of another's occupation at
the top takes me to the battleground in
my mind, grown bloodier with time -
yes, no, maybe I'll just dissolve and
melt into the carpet where I stand, or
I'll get dizzy and fall and feel my heart
snap into two and understand that I'll
never amount to anything in life.
The strife between logic and the stupid
want but need to be the best.

It's my worst fear, being the second best.

Time

It flies like the tissue in the wind,
as if it were not worth a single penny.

Each second on the clock
sucks us into the malevolent trap
that is thinking seconds mean nothing -
each a speck of dust on a shelf seen only
when the years have passed,
when it has fallen on your cheeks,
and drawn over your skin.

It flies so quickly, so shamelessly,
as if there were infinity for us all.

A fathom, an illusion, tricking us
into thinking we have any at all.

Age of Aquarius

There is not a second to be,
a second to feel the moment.

Always running ahead,
just getting it done with.

The limit of proportionality
has been reached and
nothing will ever go back
to how it used it be.

The future is now and
I have to think fast.

Plan my path as if there
truly was tomorrow
and tomorrow each day
for the Age of Aquarius
is dawning and change
is all there will be.

Arrow

5

It strikes and I fall,
I shake and I lose it all -
A tree, no branches.

Lost

That day, I left me.

I didn't know who I was,
for I was a shell -
only an arrow
defined me at that moment.

I was a question.

Seize

In a blink,

others' lips make the sounds
                I used to recognise,
   the words I no longer
              under stand the words
   I can't prononouce with
                 frag ment ed sounds
sliding off tongue
                 and twitching huk
    pulling corner of mouth
 into half smile
                and it doesn't make sense
     with the arrow
lingerr ing   scarrring
              taunting me
     with the arrival of
                 the ele ct rical de vil,

but it all fades and I'm left alone.

Beasts Left Behind

Nothing can rid the beasts
that the arrow brought along:
the beasts that strike
on the brightest days.

They open the door with
their slithering tongues,
striking where they shouldn't,
painting over my eyes with grey,
forcing the chain around my tongue.

But until the day comes,
when the arrow is torn out from above,
these beasts will devour me -
chew my mind like chewing gum
and spit me out as the bloodied saliva
clears away, clearing my eyes
to reveal a clear world,
as if nothing had happened.

Aftermath

9

It flew and pierced through
the source of all the words
that tell the stories behind my eyes,
the words that fall from
between my lips and into my hands.

A weakening beat fell silent
as the power was cut.
The last sparks faded
as my lips fell shut,
and my hands fell limp.

Not a sound, hands empty,
nothing to be told in a mind
that used to be full of things to say.

Bucket

I take the mind from my brain,
and drop it in a bucket on the sand.

I strike a match and smell the
sulphur in the air, feeling the heat
scrape my nail as I chuck the stick,
a metallic ring sounding over
the crash and sizzle of the waves.

I walk a metre away,
and I sit on the sand.

My knees cradled in my hands,
the fire in my eyes.

I let myself go,
and I watch
myself
burn.

Don't Count On It

I once had a plan,
for a holiday or an event,
for a class or a future.

There was no time
to run and guess,
to play and make a mess
I could clean up after:

there was a future at stake.

It took more than last-minute changes
or unreceived applications
to place me on the right rail.

It took a train to run over my health
and everything I had ever planned.

The Search

Among the black sky and the ocean of my mind,
the vivid dreams and the waves of thoughts,
I search for answers in the night.

But my questions seem to go unanswered,
whispered into the air, scattering across
existence,
getting lost among the echoes of answers
to others' prayers and cries long sought.

I wait and wade across the shore,
compelled to swim and float still,
ears under the water, taking it all in.

Perhaps there lie the answers,
the solutions and rhetorical questions
to place my feet on the ground where
I will walk the path meant for me.

Past the rivers of my tears
and the streams of my sweat,
it might lead to the fruition of my dreams,
the fruits of the seeds I've sown.

So perhaps there I shall go,
when the tide draws in at the right time.

Return

The present moment could not be more perfect,
but though the wound has healed, the scar
remains.

When the time comes and a beast comes out to
play,
I still walk with déjà vu, the panic in my
collarbone,
the vibrating heart and legs with no bones.

I know the arrow is still there,
but by the grace of something divine,
I almost forget until I see the fog
and hear the beasts whispering again.

Golden Blue

A milky blanket of blue,
lays neatly across the
palace above our heads.

A giant mine of gold
lights the earth each day:
clouds with bright halos
and delicate rays that plate
our breath with gold.

I melt into the grass
and I watch it all pass
as I think about the past,
on the brink of freedom, at last.

Sunshine

15

The sun's sweet whispers,
A soft tickle on the cheek -
The dark days are gone.

Electric

I feel hammers wrecking chains just welded,
spiders weaving webs of titanium,
bullets firing, arrows shooting,
and I'm thriving in the thrill of it all.

With the sparks in place
of the twinkle in my eye,
the thunderbolts in place of my veins,
I am indestructible through
the divine chaos of it all.

Water

I still feel the beasts,
through the sun and rain, but now,
I hope and wait like

calm ocean waters,
the dancing shimmers waiting
for me to join in.

The Moral

The air feels crisp again,
my breath finally feels easier,
and the world glows a little brighter.

My mind feels like a world
I've longed to see since I
don't even remember when.

My heart is overflowing:
a cup of tea with a little too
much honey added in.

The lesson has been taught,
the realisation has hit,
and no shame is to be felt.

The arrow flew and struck
the target, and now it sits in place,
ready to release the beasts at the sight of
worried brows and itineraries.

An alarm, a trigger, a guardian
that taught me the power of the moment
and the value of the wait.

* 9 7 8 9 3 5 8 3 1 3 0 9 3 *